What others are saying about this book:

"This book is a must read. It is fundamental to understanding the sales process and will help someone dramatically improve sales results. The ideas in this book represent the difference between success and failure in today's world."

— Matt Golden, Senior VP Sales, Navigant International

"Exceedingly clever! At last, a new idea in sales education. Sell Little Red Hen! Sell! is an original, a "keeper"! This is a great way to teach and reinforce sales basics and principles!"

— Lloyd Tucker, Senior Director, DMIA

"Jeffrey Hansler has written a wonderful story that shows you how to sell. His engaging and memorable story keeps you turning the pages and leaves you with vivid learning tools. This book belongs on the desk of everyone."

— Steve Kaye, Ph.D., Business Expert

"I loved reading this wonderful book You will embrace the Little Red Hen as she becomes your guide to making the impossible - possible. It is a book that will make a tremendous difference in your life."

— Glenna Salsbury, CSP, CPAE,
Speaker Hall of Fame,
Author of <u>The Art of the Fresh Start</u>,
and Professional Speaker

Sell
Little Red Hen!
Sell!

Jeffrey Hansler

First Edition

AP Advantage Publishing Inc.
Fountain Valley, CA

Acknowledgements

I wish to thank all those that contributed their time to making this book happen.

For all the editing time and struggling through initial drafts, I wish to thank Harriet Carter, Glenna Salsbury, David Dworski, Sue Podany, Kay Baum, Raymond Obstfeld, Cynthia David, and Susie DeWeese.

To experts in the field and their works: Thea Alexander, Og Mandino, Arthur Miller, Roger Dawson, Charlie Jones, Dr. Carl Jung, Dr. Milton H. Erickson, Dr. Abraham Maslow, Richard Bandler, Dr. John Grinder, Brian Tracy, David Sandler, Tom Hopkins, Jack Canfield, Dr. Spencer Johnson, and of course Putnam Books for *The Little Red Hen*.

Dedication

This book is dedicated to Mackenzie and Riley...

... and to anyone that has wanted to contribute and thrive in a world they didn't understand.

I'm excited about the journey on which you are ready to embark. The learning concepts are skillfully layered within the story, and you will experience the lessons the book has to offer even before you are even aware of the process. *Sell Little Red Hen! Sell!* is a breakthrough in sales learning that you will appreciate long after you put the book down.

Roger Dawson, Speaker, Author of
Secrets of Power Negotiating

Introduction

Why Should I Read This Book?

This book is your guide to selling even if you don't think of yourself as being in the profession of selling.

If it bothers you to be associated with the profession of selling then you will likely want to disagree with this next statement:

Nothing gets done until someone sells someone on getting it done.

The common disagreement to this statement is if you can do it yourself, you do not need to have sales skills. The question is *'Did someone sell you on this idea?'*

Face it, in today's environment if you want your ideas implemented, you'll likely need someone's cooperation, which will require persuasive communication skills. There are many great ideas, but the ones that finally get implemented have effective salespeople behind them – even if these people don't wear the title of professional salesperson.

What if a doctor has the cure for a patient, but the treatment will cost more than the HMO or the insurance company is willing to pay? Who will change their mind if the procedure is considered experimental? The life of the patient may be dependent on the ability of someone to be good in sales. That someone could be you!

What if you're an engineer and you believe that a structure requires additional support because of unique seismic findings, but neither building codes nor the builder support your conclusions? How many lives might depend on your ability to sell your idea?

What if you want to convince a child not to call a dog across the street through traffic? You get the picture.

If your response is "It's not my job... It's out of my control...I tried to tell them", that's one option for you. Another option for you is to view each of these situations as an opportunity to use persuasive skills.

I believe that our use of persuasive skills makes this a better world to live in for everyone. Find the greatest accomplishments that have been made to the world and you'll find someone behind them with a persuasive ability.

Not so long ago, my problem was that I didn't know how to be effectively persuasive. Then I had a personal "discovery" that unlocked the key to understanding effective persuasion.

I had been through about every sales class there was prior to my discovery of the key to sales. From these early sales classes, I had learned strategies, phrases, and techniques, because that's what they taught. But just because you put your four-year-old behind the wheel of a car, does not mean you've given the child the ability to drive. They have a tool - the car, but no knowledge of how to use that tool. The key is to understand the basic principles of how we act, respond and make decisions as human beings. Unless you understand these principles, all the strategies, phrases, and techniques will be of no use to you.

The purpose of this book is to provide you a perspective that delivers to you the key principles to understanding selling. This book prepares you to understand the essence of selling, thus providing you with the ability of guiding someone to a decision.

Why is there a negative connotation to selling?

Not long after my discovery moment, I became involved in the business of education. While conducting sales and negotiation classes, I often am asked questions like:

Why is there often a poor perception of the profession of sales and salespeople in general?

Why are people afraid I'll be pushy once they find out I'm in sales?

Aren't salespeople a dime a dozen?

I believe these questions are asked because people intuitively understand the value of learning to sell while having personally experienced disturbing examples of sales execution.

I explain to my audiences that possibly 90% of the salespeople out there have no idea of what selling is all about. The majority of individuals in sales did not intend to be in sales. It just became a means to an end for them. Some solve their 'sales issues' with aggressive behavior, tricks, slick presentations, and withholding information. These are the individuals (and organizations) that give sales a bad name. Their concept of selling is that someone is a winner and someone is a loser. They can be pushy, aggressive, and downright threatening. It's not a pretty picture. You won't see this trait in someone who truly understands sales.

Others solve their 'sales issues' by coasting along. They survive on the top ten percent's crumbs and the momentum successful salespeople bring to their organization. They are not willing to put in the hard work required to be successful – whether or not they represent the "best" product or service. The results they yield are disappointing and lead to the negative perceptions of sales and salespeople reflected by the questions above, including *salespeople are a dime a dozen*.

Is hard work the answer to selling successfully?

Some of those *pushy* salespeople believe that being aggressive is just part of the hard work required to be successful in sales.

Others work hard in different ways. They work hard to give customers whatever they want. They work long hours and long weeks to make sure that their customers are completely taken care of.

Is that the answer? Well, it's one answer and I should know, because I was one of those who approached sales in this manner. I can accurately say that the majority of my success in the early days of my career was due to hard work – not sales skills. And if hard work wouldn't get me the sale, I lost it, because I didn't want to be that *pushy* salesperson.

Here's the problem. If your company has a clearly superior product, fantastic value, or has a track record of getting the job done at an unbelievably lower price than anyone else, you can be successful in sales without great sales skills. This can be done by putting more work into the process of selling – spending longer hours, sending out more information, meeting more people and a host of other sales activities. There are individuals and organizations in sales that do not have the personal sales skills necessary, but who do well because they have a strategic advantage created by their company, and they work hard to make sure everyone knows they have a strategic advantage and superior offer.

Ask yourself these questions, *What if I don't have a strategic advantage? What if my company had the best product, but now there is a new competitor who can do it better and cheaper? How can I sell now?* These questions can be frightening to consider if you're the one that must supply the answers.

What would you do if your company didn't have a strategic advantage or superior offer? Should you quit? (*Sometimes I did.*) Go work for the competition? (*I did this, too.*)

Is your life going to be filled with constant job-hunting for the perfect product or service company to work for? (*Yes, I did this, too.*) Maybe you can survive by working even harder. (*I did this when I had no other option.*) If there were enough other people on our team working extremely hard, then the company would survive, which means you'd probably survive as well.

Is there a better way?

I was often told so by sales managers and company owners, "Work hard and you can be a success in sales."

The truth is, hard work helps, but it's not the key to sales. In fact, if you look around the best salespeople seem to make sales look effortless. Specifically, you may not even identify them as salespeople. They might be surgeons, lawyers, teachers, supervisors, religious leaders, presidents, senators, parents, or even your neighbors.

In the profession of selling, the top 10% in sales seem to have an understanding the lower 90% are lacking. They understand that being part of the top group can't be accomplished by hard work alone. To reach the top requires an understanding of sales at a different cognitive level. The problem for the rest of us is that not many of the top 10% can explain how they do what they do. When you ask them about their success, the response is generally a platitude, "I worked hard, worked smart, and got lucky."

The purpose of this book is to let you in on the secret of what they do differently, and to provide you a different cognitive understanding of sales.

"I have been to a dozen sales classes before, why did I finally 'get it' from this class?" is a question I am asked after someone has attended one of my sales classes, and the main reason I wrote this book.

The answer to the question is simple: I have traveled this road. I have experienced the limits of hard work, suffered the disastrous results of not having an understanding of sales, and I was finally guided to a place where I could learn what only a few salespeople know: There is an essence to selling! There is a different cognitive understanding, a *key* that comes only after someone has internalized specific principles. I will share these principles with you through the Little Red Hen's journey.

Why is the book written like a children's story?

As a parent, I rediscovered something I took for granted as a child. I enjoyed the simple ideas children's books conveyed. Simple ideas make it easy to focus. I also rediscovered that big lessons for life are often contained in simple ideas.

What better way to keep the big lesson simple than to demonstrate it through a children's story? This format kept me from adding too much detail and becoming distracted from the basic concepts that started me down the right path of my sales journey. Becoming sidetracked is what I feel has happened to many types of sales training and sales training literature. The ever-compounding details included in training bog down the primary purpose of training. This primary purpose is to create an understanding of sales by having individuals experience the discovery of selling.

There is another reason I choose a children's story format. When we were children, we were in a conscious and constant state of learning. It wasn't an option since there was so much that we didn't know. Sometimes as adults, we have such high expectations of ourselves that at some point we forget we had to learn and practice to become proficient.

One of the greatest **myths** out there is that -

Great salespeople are born salespeople.

The truth is that salespeople have all learned their craft, though some good salespeople are not fully aware of how and where they learned their craft. They may give the impression that they were "born" that way.

Maybe they grew up in a selling environment. A famous software founder grew up in such an environment. Though he may not think of himself as such, he really is a great salesperson. He learned his skills at an early age from his home environment. When you consider his parents and what they did for a living, it's easy to realize that "born salespeople" are just people born in a house where excellent and persuasive communicators abound.

Maybe it was not their parents, but an uncle, a cousin, a friend or a teacher that was able to model for them the behaviors that make a good salesperson. In short, if you are not good at sales, it's not because you can't do it, it's because you haven't had proper sales models in your life.

If you don't have such models in your life, you simply won't be able to internalize the sales process. This may explain to you why you haven't been as successful as you could have been in selling, even after learning sales verbiage and techniques.

Without internalizing the sales process, you won't think on a level of persuasion or feel the thought process of someone making a decision. It is similar to the difference between you shooting a basketball (or ice skating or whatever) and Michael Jordan (or some other master of their profession) shooting a basketball: your shot is missing the magic ingredient that goes beyond the intellectual knowledge of good practice and becomes that magical internalized process.

Every aspect of this book was chosen to give you that magic ingredient to help you sell. The book was written to create a model for you that would open for you the sealed door of sales.

I used the model of a children's story because I wanted to access the models you developed while growing up. I have created a time machine in your mind that allows us to go back and give you a second opportunity to integrate new learning into your past so that it will be ingrained and available to you in the future.

The answers to selling are placed in this book so that your childhood mind could play with them before your adult mind said "NO". This is a book in which you'll make a new discovery each time you read it.

I have done everything I could in this book to guide you on your journey to learn selling and master it.

The world of selling is a fabulous world full of growth and learning. If you have a negative perception of sales, it could be because there are many people with the title of sales, but without the heart, and without the magic ingredient. They are in sales, not by choice, but because they couldn't do or didn't do what they really wanted to do, and they don't appreciate the opportunity they have.

Why did I choose the Little Red Hen as my main character?

I choose the Little Red Hen because the lesson of this children's book is "If you work hard, you will earn the rewards in life."

This lesson seems much less true now than it has ever been in the past. There are too many people that work very hard, yet never get their deserved reward. There are too many people that work hard and have only limited success.

I believe that someone who is willing to work hard should reap enormous rewards.

If you didn't read <u>The Little Red Hen</u>, or did and forgot the storyline, here's a brief synopsis:

The Little Red Hen wanted to make some bread for herself and her chicks and anyone else that would help. She asked for help from several other barnyard animals, but they all refused. So she ended up cutting the wheat, grinding it up, making the dough, gathering the wood for the fire, and tending to the baking of the bread. Once the bread was made, all the animals that she had asked for help showed up to eat the bread, which the Little Red Hen denied to them. The ending of the story was "I did all the work, you did not help me, I will eat all the bread and you will get none." The moral of the story is that if you work hard you will get the reward, and if you don't work hard – you won't.

Or at least that's the moral as it was explained to me. For many years, 21 years to be exact, I guided my sales actions by that message: I will work hard and I will eat. The problem was that in the business world, working hard didn't always work. In fact, there were many times I worked hard and was not given credit, or even worse, was not paid for my hard work. The final straw occurred when ... well that's another story.

What I have come to realize is that the Little Red Hen was asking for help by asking the wrong questions in the wrong way. She would ask an animal, 'Will you help me cut the wheat? Will you help me grind the wheat? Will you help me heat the oven?'

Are you surprised that the answer was "No!"? She was surprised and disappointed. She couldn't understand why they did not see the benefit of helping.

Her thought process was self-centered. Of course, the answer would be no, because her focus was on the steps of the process of making bread and result that was important to her. She never talked about the benefit to those that would be helping her.

So how do we get the Little Red Hen to see things from outside her current perspective? I pick up the story of the Little Red Hen many years after she first baked the bread for her chicks and take her on a journey that provides her a new experience and the skills to operate in an entirely new world. It's a journey where she learns the skills to persuade others to help her. The concepts are universal and apply to all situations, so it will apply to your products, services and ideas.

Please join the Little Red Hen on her journey. I am confident that after reading her story you will agree that there is no one better to help you to understanding the essence of sales through questions than the Little Red Hen. She will help you realize from her own discovery that hard work alone won't solve problems.

How important are questions to understanding sales?

In Arthur Miller's play, *Death of a Salesman*, to get insurance money for his family, Willie Loweman commits suicide by crashing his car after realizing he had never been a salesperson – just a person masquerading as one.

He worked hard, but without a true understanding of sales. The real sadness is that he could have been a great salesman – if he'd only asked the critical questions to internalize the process of sales. Questions are a key to understanding and implementing sales at all levels.

My hope is that this book will help you find the questions you need to ask to become a great salesperson – whether or not you wear that title as part of your work.

If you're worried that you may actually learn the essence of selling from a children's story, you may not want to read this book, because this book may change your life forever...if you let it.

Sell
Little Red Hen!

Sell!

The Little Red Hen Wakes Up to a Different World

With a letter in her hand, the Little Red Hen was sitting in her kitchen at her pine farm table - a table where she and her little chicks had eaten many hearty meals made from scratch by her. Now she was alone.

Her chicks had left and made homes of their own. Though sad, she knew they would visit and now was the time she could relax and enjoy the coming years in peaceful, quiet security. That was, until the letter arrived yesterday from her lawyer and financial advisor, Mr. Rat.

Her nest egg of investments that she had worked so hard to earn and save were gone, lost by poor management and a vicious turn in the market that swept everything away. Poor Little Red Hen!

How would she replace it? She couldn't rebuild it the same way she originally did. She had worked so hard for so many years to earn that money. She wouldn't even be able to bake enough bread to keep her peaceful little home. The world had changed so much she wasn't even sure her baking skills were competitive in today's economy.

"Yes, times had certainly changed," thought the Little Red Hen.

It was no longer a matter of going down and cutting wheat and baking a loaf of bread. It had always been hard to get good help, even back then. Now it seemed nearly impossible to the Little Red Hen to make a living, let alone make enough money to replace her financial nest egg.

This question had been on her mind since the letter arrived. It was her most pressing thought as she sat at the kitchen table.

"How will I replace my nest egg?" thought the Little Red Hen.

She thought about the mule across the way. He had lost his job a year ago and was still out of work. He refused to look for another type of work or even change how he sought out similar work. He certainly was stubborn.

The Little Red Hen thought about the beaver in the river at the edge of the barnyard. The beaver was proficient at what she did, but she was barely making ends meet. It seemed that it didn't matter if you were talented at what you could do, you still might not get a fair wage for your efforts.

Or worse, she thought about the hens in the hen house. They were forced to work long and hard. No matter how long or how hard they had worked, if they stopped producing, they were replaced with another hen. It didn't seem right, but then that's the way it was in today's world (out of the hen house and into the frying pan). These thoughts were very troubling to the Little Red Hen.

The Little Red Hen still didn't have any answers by the time the mail came that afternoon. To tell the truth, the Little Red Hen was a little nervous about getting her mail; she wasn't up to more awful surprises.

"Well, it's not going to go away," she said aloud as she rose to get the mail.

No big surprises fortunately: the usual junk mail, bills, and her magazines. There was even a real estate sales flier from her realtor, Ms. Peacock, listing a house by the pond. That was a laugh! Her being able to purchase a house by the pond. She was battling her fears just to figure out a way to keep her little home.

She thought about Ms. Peacock.

Ms. Peacock had sold the Little Red Hen her house a long time ago. She was a successful realtor and appeared to love her job. She had one of the biggest houses in the barnyard, and she seemed to have time on her hands to enjoy herself. The Little Red Hen thought, "If only I could sell real estate, then I would not have any worries at all."

Then it hit her. She could sell real estate. "How hard could it be?" she said to herself. "After all, I know what I like in a house, and the rest is just paperwork."

The Little Red Hen decided right then and there "That's it, I will sell real estate!" With that decision, she stood a little firmer and smoothed her feathers in the mirror.

I can make a lot of money in a short time and meet lots of people," she concluded.

It didn't seem to matter to the Little Red Hen that she had never sold real estate before. She was excited about the possibilities. And if she couldn't sell real estate, she would sell something else. Sales looked easy. Anyone could do it.

"No time like the present," thought the Little Red Hen, and off she went to see Ms. Peacock.

The Little Red Hen Talks with Ms. Peacock

The Little Red Hen was very excited. She thought about all the people that needed houses and all the beautiful houses out there to be sold. Why, if everything went as planned, she might even get herself a new home – maybe even a home by the pond.

On her way to Ms. Peacock's, she was stopped by some of the other barnyard animals. "Where are you going?" they asked.

"To see Ms. Peacock about learning to sell houses," replied the Little Red Hen.

"You can't do that!" they all laughed.

Ms. Squirrel said, "You've never done that before," and scampered off, laughing as she looked for nuts to store away.

"You're too nice," Mr. Weasel laughed in her face.

"What do you know about houses?" said Ms. Beaver, who couldn't even stop working to talk as she put another stick on the dam she was repairing.

It seemed everyone had something to say about the Little Red Hen's impending doom. At first, she didn't worry, but as more animals told her she couldn't do it, the more the Little Red Hen began to believe it herself.

By the time the Little Red Hen arrived at Ms. Peacock's house she was very discouraged. In fact, she felt worse than when she'd realized her financial troubles. Not only did she still have money worries, now she was convinced that she had just lost a chance to help herself.

"Who am I kidding? I can't sell!" she thought. She turned to leave before even opening the garden gate to Ms. Peacock's home.

As she slowly walked away, an ounce of fear and a cup of courage crept into her thoughts, "I really have no choice. I must do this even if I fail. How else am I going to rebuild my financial nest egg?"

With that, the Little Red Hen opened the gate and marched up the brick path onto the front porch and right up to the large elegant front door.

The Little Red Hen paused before she knocked. She was second-guessing herself again. "The animals were probably right."

"Yes, they are most definitely right," she almost said aloud. She turned to leave for good this time.

Before the Little Red Hen was even off the porch, the door opened and out stepped Ms. Peacock. "Well, hello Little Red Hen. How are you?"

The Little Red Hen was so surprised that she blurted out in a strained and high-pitched voice, "I want to sell houses!"

Ms. Peacock smiled; she liked the Little Red Hen. She knew the Little Red Hen to be earnest, hardworking, and persistent. She also knew she had no experience selling. She also knew that the Little Red Hen must be worried about something to be at her door in this state of mind.

Ms. Peacock reached out with a warm smile and replied, "That is a marvelous idea. Why don't you come in and we'll talk about it?"

Ms. Peacock's smile and gentle supportive response picked up the spirits of the Little Red Hen. She followed Ms. Peacock into the house, a beautiful house with lots of fine furniture and comfortable places to sit. The Little Red Hen looked at all the beautiful things and longingly said, "Your home is so wonderful."

"Why thank you, Little Red Hen", replied Ms. Peacock. "Please sit down while I get us something to eat and drink."

After getting them a snack, Ms. Peacock asked questions and listened as the Little Red Hen talked.

Ms. Peacock noticed that, as the Little Red Hen answered her questions and shared her idea, she became excited once again about the idea of selling houses.

To the grateful Little Red Hen, Ms. Peacock seemed to hang onto every word and show genuine interest in the answers. The normally private Little Red Hen shared her worries and the fear of losing her cozy home. She tried to hide her tears until she saw the caring in Ms. Peacock's eyes.

The room was silent except for the ticking grandfather clock and the Little Red Hen's sobs. Ms. Peacock held the Little Red Hen until there were no more tears to fall.

Finally, as the Little Red Hen dried her eyes, Ms. Peacock asked her one last question. "Do you think if you could sell houses, you could sell anything?"

The Little Red Hen hadn't thought of that. "Why, yes I do," said the Little Red Hen after some consideration.

"Good," said Ms. Peacock "and while there are some differences, I agree. If you could successfully sell houses, with some work you could sell anything. So may I make a suggestion to you?"

"Why... yes," said the Little Red Hen.

"I would like you to learn to sell with a product that has a shorter buying cycle," said Ms. Peacock with authority, "because learning to sell is one thing and selling a particular product in a particular area is another."

"I have many colleagues that are not as successful as I am, not because they don't know houses, but because they don't know selling." Ms. Peacock continued with carefully chosen words. She knew much more about the Little Red Hen and how the Little Red Hen pictured ideas than the Little Red Hen even knew about herself.

"Do you see and believe the difference?" asked Ms. Peacock.

"Why... yes," said the Little Red Hen as she thought about Mr. Badger, who worked very hard to sell houses, and wasn't good at all.

"Good. You should find great security in this knowledge," said Ms. Peacock.

Ms. Peacock continued, "If you really want to learn to sell, go and see Mr. Rooster. He has a company where you can learn to sell."

"After you have gained the security of learning to sell, you will enter into the world of successful sales. I like to think of it as a selling family. Then you can come back to me, and we will talk about selling houses. Is that OK?" asked Ms. Peacock.

Although the Little Red Hen was disappointed because her vision of selling houses seemed delayed, it also gave her hope, because it was obvious Ms. Peacock believed she could sell. "Yes, I can accept that," replied the Little Red Hen. With that, she thanked her hostess and headed out to see Mr. Rooster, because there was no time like the present.

As the Little Red Hen walked away, Ms. Peacock smiled because she knew that if the Little Red Hen was willing to open herself up to learning, she would be coming back to visit her with a sense of security that she had never known before.

The Little Red Hen Goes to See Mr. Rooster

Mr. Rooster sat in his well-worn, big leather chair behind his large polished office desk. The gray in his feathers added to his presence. The rich wood paneling and plush carpet conveyed the success that Mr. Rooster wanted conveyed. His demeanor was calm, organized, and kind.

As the Little Red Hen sat in his office telling her story, Mr. Rooster knew that she had a long row to hoe. He was glad that she had gone to see Ms. Peacock, one of the few who really understood selling. He also thought it was more than just coincidence that the Little Red Hen picked Ms. Peacock to visit.

After the Little Red Hen finished, he asked her how he could help.

"I would like to work for you in sales," she said with a small but convicted voice.

"There are many things you don't know about selling and you have no experience," said Mr. Rooster bluntly.

As she heard these words, the Little Red Hen felt the pit in her stomach grow. Inside, her heart dropped and her head visibly bowed.

"And," continued Mr. Rooster, "there are many qualities you have that will aid you in sales." He paused.

'Did I hear words of hope?' the Little Red Hen said to herself. 'Is he going to give me a chance?'

Mr. Rooster continued, "So, yes, I will hire you. On one condition!"

She was so excited that she would have agreed to anything. "Yes, what is it?"

Mr. Rooster was hiring the Little Red Hen based on her previous success with baking the bread. She had a can-do attitude. He liked that.

Being a wise Old Rooster, he knew that without past experience, she could not learn in the office what she needed to know. He'd put her on the road, knowing she'd sink or swim – so to speak. "You start tomorrow and you don't come into my office again until the end of the week."

She was shocked. 'Start tomorrow – and not see him until the end of the week!' There would be no one to help her. She knew there must be so much to learn – even if sales was easy!

She was going to say something and then she thought, "He must know what he is doing since he's been so successful."

"I agree," said the Little Red Hen after long consideration, and before Mr. Rooster could say anything else she excused herself because she had much work to do.

"Yes", thought Mr. Rooster as she walked out of his office. "She has a can-do attitude."

On her way out of his office, the Little Red Hen was already in high gear. She grabbed information about the products – there was so much. She got technical manuals and specs and all kinds of other material and information to help her learn about the products.

As she left, laden with all the product information she could carry, the Rooster watched her, smiled, shook his head and thought. "Yes, the Little Red Hen had a long row to hoe."

The Little Red Hen
Calls on Mr. Horse

That night she stayed up late and studied. The candle burned until the early hours of the morning. When the rooster crowed and the new day began, she was tired and excited at the same time.

She knew she couldn't learn everything, so she focused on the products that she liked. These would be the ones she'd learn the most about so she could tell everyone about them.

At 6 o'clock a.m. a fax arrived. It was from Mr. Rooster. It said that she was to call on Mr. Horse at 10 o'clock a.m. - sharp. The fax stated that Mr. Horse had previously purchased from Mr. Rooster and was now interested in more products.

"This is great," she thought. "This will be easy. I don't even need to find buyers for these products." And upstairs she went to get ready for her first sales appointment. With time to spare, she was soon off to the corral to meet Mr. Horse.

Arriving on time and neatly dressed, she introduced herself to Mr. Horse and stated that she was representing Mr. Rooster's company.

Despite the fact that Mr. Horse looked a bit rigid and non-talkative, she started talking about how great the company was and all the products and services that might be of interest to Mr. Horse. She was giving him everything she had learned during the night.

Mr. Horse tried to speak several times, but the Little Red Hen talked right through his attempts to interrupt her verbal presentation.

The Little Red Hen had learned a great deal of product information during the night and went on for some time.

Mr. Horse had a very strong desire to redirect the Little Red Hen and get control of the situation. He contained himself with much restraint.

Finally, after what seemed a lifetime to Mr. Horse, the Little Red Hen stopped to take a breath. He quickly and politely interrupted and asked, "Would you like to know what I'm interested in?"

"Of course," she said without missing a beat. "That's why I'm here, but I just thought you'd also like to know about everything else as well."

"Frankly, " said Mr. Horse, "it's too much information for me to handle. What I want is this," he said pointing to a product brochure that was laid out in a pile on his desk. "I believe it will give me the extra accomplishment I want."

The Little Red Hen was ecstatic, in her mind a sale was on the horizon. It was one of the products she had picked to focus on. "That is a great choice, Mr. Horse," said the Little Red Hen pointing to the brochure, "that product does this and this, but you get this and this which are its best features. I love this product for this reason and this reason, but you may like it for other reasons."

"I'm not much interested in the things you have been talking about," said Mr. Horse. "How much does it cost?" he asked.

"It is this much," said the Little Red Hen pointing to the price list, "but that's for the basic model."

"That's too much," stated Mr. Horse. "Thank you for coming." With that he ushered her out the door.

In seconds, she found herself outside his office with a messy briefcase and a confused look on her face and, of course, no sale!

As she walked home, she thought of everything that happened. She liked the product, she knew the information about the product, and she gave him everything she brought with her.

What had gone wrong? She reflected on what Mr. Horse had said. Then it dawned on her. He said that she had given him too much information. He must have been confused. After all, he was just a horse, and not very friendly at all.

"What an idiot I was for overloading him," thought the Little Red Hen.

She was disappointed at losing her first opportunity for a sale. She thought long and hard on what could she do next time so they wouldn't be confused. She could make a presentation. She could put together pictures and charts that explained how the product worked. "That's it! I need a presentation to give."

She hurried the rest of the way home to get working on her presentation. As she walked, she muttered to herself, "If Mr. Rooster had given me some help, maybe I could have had a presentation made and this wouldn't have happened and maybe my feet wouldn't hurt from all this walking."

After stomping a few strides, she acknowledged her negative thought process and set it aside. "Mr. Rooster knows what he is doing and he is doing the things that will help me succeed, but my feet still hurt."

When she arrived there was another fax from Mr. Rooster. It said she was supposed to see Ms. Pig tomorrow and mentioned the specific product that Ms. Pig wanted to see.

This was great. Now she could work all night on doing a perfect presentation for Ms. Pig on the product she wanted.

The Little Red Hen Calls on Ms. Pig

Armed with her presentation, the Little Red Hen marched into the pigpen where Ms. Pig had a nice snack waiting and some songbirds singing on the fence railing in the background.

"Welcome to my space," said Ms. Pig with a smile. Ms. Pig was very proud of her pigpen and how cozy it was for guests to relax and talk. "Mr. Rooster said we could spend some time getting to know each other and you could tell me all about the product. Would you like a snack first?"

"No, thank you, Ms. Pig. I put a presentation together, and I'm excited to show it to you."

"Well, OK," said Ms. Pig hiding her disappointment.

And with that, the Little Red Hen pushed aside the pictures of all Ms. Pig's children and grandchildren, put her equipment on the table and dove into her presentation.

It had color and excitement and pizzazz – the Little Red Hen felt that barnyard had never experienced such a presentation – it must be simply marvelous. She even noticed the songbirds on the fence watching her run through her presentation for Ms. Pig. "Yes," thought the Little Red Hen. "This is going to be a sale."

And, as she reached the end, the Little Red Hen asked, "So how many would you like?" She had learned this approach from an audiotape on selling that she had listened to while creating her presentation for Ms. Pig.

"Well, it all sounds wonderful," said Ms. Pig "Are you sure you don't want to nibble on something now that your presentation is over?"

"No, thank you, Ms. Pig," said the Little Red Hen, at which point Ms. Pig's phone rang.

"Excuse me for a moment," said Ms. Pig, as she headed to the phone.

When she hung up, Ms. Pig apologized and said, "I'm sorry, I must go. It sounds like Ms. Hog needs some help at the office and I really should assist her. We have such a great relationship."

"In any case, I usually talk with Ms. Hog before I make a decision anyway. So thank you and just let yourself out once you pack your presentation. Don't worry about straightening up. I will do that when I get back. Good-bye." Ms. Pig said as she quickly disappeared down the lane to Ms. Hog's, leaving a very stunned Little Red Hen. The Little Red Hen packed up her presentation and put the picture frames back in their place without noticing any faces.

Once again the Little Red Hen was walking back to her home without a sale. She showed Ms. Pig a great presentation; Ms. Pig even said so.

"What went wrong?" thought the concerned Little Red Hen. Her feet hurt even more than yesterday.

The Little Red Hen was still wondering when she walked into her home and found a fax from Mr. Rooster for her next appointment.

She was to meet Mr. Duck at the pond, located at the third log from the oak tree center point, tomorrow at 9 o'clock a.m. – sharp. He wanted three brochures on a particular product, pricing, and a short presentation of four slides showing the main benefits of the product. He had fourteen minutes and 25 seconds for the meeting. His number was listed. If she had any questions on the meeting place, she could call Mr. Duck.

She was certain she knew the location, so why call and appear to be unsure.

As she thought about his request for a very brief presentation, she wondered how she could excite Mr. Duck about the products. She had to tell him about the benefits of the products.

A flash went off in the Little Red Hen's mind. That must have been the problem with her presentation to Ms. Pig. The Little Red Hen hadn't included benefits of the product. She had just talked about the features, which the audiotape program had explained were not as important as the benefits of what the products could do for the buyers.

So she would get ready for Mr. Duck and have an entire list of benefits just for him.

The Little Red Hen Calls on Mr. Duck

She got confused at the pond! There were, in fact, two oak trees in the area that led to entirely different logs. Unfortunately, you couldn't directly see the logs from either oak tree because of the tall cattails in between – so it was pick one and hope.

At 8:59 a.m., by her watch, she ran from the log where she was to the other log worrying that she must have chosen the wrong one, but there was no sign of Mr. Duck at the second log either.

She waited a minute and then ran back to the first log on very sore feet and there found Mr. Duck waiting impatiently. He looked at his watch briefly and then asked her if she brought what he asked for.

She presented to him the material in a notebook.

"Thank you," Mr. Duck said. "Very efficient. Now can you tell me what peace of mind I will have if I buy this product?"

The Little Red Hen showed him pictures of other's excitement about using the product. She showed him letters from other customers bragging about how the product changed their lives. She talked about how he would be perceived as a great guy and well liked if he had this product. All the benefits she had discovered that others had gained from this product.

When she was through, she asked him for the order and she shut up, because she had learned about this technique from the audiotape program too.

After what seemed like a long pause, Mr. Duck said, "Thank you for coming. I will review this information and if I have any more questions, I will call you and set up an appointment to discuss it." With that, off he swam. It was 9:14 and 25 seconds according to her watch.

Once again, she was dumbfounded. What had happened? She gave him everything he wanted and loaded the conversation with benefits and still no order.

She began to wonder if everyone was right about her. Maybe she wasn't capable of selling. Maybe it was too late to learn. Maybe Mr. Rooster didn't spend any time with her because he knew she would fail. She walked home rather depressed.

As she entered her home, the silence deepened her depression. She slumped into the overstuffed chair by the empty fireplace. She was failing terribly and everyone would soon know it. She would lose her home and have to live with the other chickens in the hen house. How did she ever get herself into this mess?

Feeling very alone, she got up to drag herself to bed, when she noticed the fax.

"Keep a positive attitude, Little Red Hen," said the note from Mr. Rooster. "I know you can do it. Go see Ms. Lizard tomorrow. She's very excited about our new product, and she has lots of money, and seems to have made up her mind. She wants you to meet her at the race track so you can answer a few simple questions for her."

"Well, this was good news," sniffed the Little Red Hen with renewed enthusiasm. "I know all about the product, so I won't have to spend all night preparing."

Mr. Rooster obviously believed in her, and so off she would go tomorrow after a good night's rest.

The Little Red Hen Calls on Ms. Lizard

The Little Red Hen loved the racetrack. It was always exciting! It was fun! What a great place to meet! She reminded herself to stay focused. She would get the sale. She found Ms. Lizard right away, yelling and cheering for her horse to win.

"Hi, Little Red Hen, glad you could make it," said Ms. Lizard. "Isn't this fun? Though not as much fun as a trip to Bermuda, eh?"

"Yes, I agree," said the Little Red Hen. "I'd give anything to be in Bermuda right now!"

"So I hear you have a great product," smiled Ms. Lizard while keeping one eye on her horse as it rounded the far corner. "Tell me about it."

The Little Red Hen told her all kinds of things about it. When Ms. Lizard asked a question or looked excited, the Little Red Hen focused her comments because she knew that was of interest to Ms. Lizard.

Ms. Lizard's horse won in the first race while they talked about all kinds of things that could be done with the product. As the next few races took place, they talked about the weather, the racing, veterinarians, good places to eat, and, of course, Bermuda. In no time at all, Ms. Lizard was asking, "How soon can I get it and how many can I get?" Well, the Little Red Hen was floored. "We just have to put together the order form and get a little more information from you. We will then get the contract to you for you to review and sign, and we could do that later today."

"Great! Let's do it," said Ms. Lizard.

With that the Little Red Hen headed to the office to get the papers and tell Mr. Rooster about her sale. Her feet didn't even bother her as she headed down the road.

The Little Red Hen
Lays an Egg – Her First Lesson

Ecstatic about her sale, she raced to Mr. Rooster.

When she arrived, he invited her in and asked how her week went.

Of course, she started off with Ms. Lizard. She talked about the sale and also how successful she had been getting Ms. Lizard excited about the product and that she had to hurry to get the papers back to her to review and sign. Beginning with this success story, thought the Little Red Hen, would save her from having to explain about the earlier part of the week's events.

Mr. Rooster smiled and he remained silent and patiently waited.

The Little Red Hen thought he must be pleased. So she felt safe enough to continue with the events involving Mr. Horse, and how the price was too high, and Ms. Pig discussing her decision with her friend, Ms. Hog, and Mr. Duck looking over the information he requested.

Actually, as she relayed the information to Mr. Rooster, she realized, it wasn't a half-bad week. Mr. Duck and Ms. Pig were thinking about it, Ms. Lizard was buying, and Mr. Horse, well, there was nothing she could do about price.

Mr. Rooster then asked an odd question, "Do you want to continue selling for us?"

She wondered why he would ask that since she had just made her first sale. In a voice somewhat shaky with concern, the Little Red Hen said, "Yes."

Mr. Rooster asked, "Why?"

"Why?" she said. "Because I love the products and services we sell, and I've just learned everything I can about them, and I know just how they will help others. I feel that I am becoming part of the selling family."

"I'm glad you want to keep selling for us, because I think you will eventually be very good. I agree with you that you are becoming part of the selling family," said Mr. Rooster with a very convincing look. "And I want you to remember that you want to keep selling. I want you to remember that I believe also that you will eventually be very good. I want you to remember that I have told you this. Will you do that?"

"Why, yes, of course," said the Little Red Hen, wondering what was coming next.

Mr. Rooster then looked at a piece of paper with notes on his desk. "Mr. Horse called Tuesday to talk with me, and tell me he was going to buy a competitor product that was cheaper, and a little more complex, but that it would help him accomplish everything he wanted.

"After talking with him for a few minutes, about the results he wanted, he became convinced that our product, the one he pointed out to you, was what he really needed, so he bought it from me at full price.

"Mr. Duck called and asked me why I sent someone who could not be on time and who did not have the information he needed to make a decision with peace of mind.

"Ms. Pig purchased another company's product from Ms. Hog. Ms. Hog is not only a friend of Ms. Pig, she is also a competitor of ours.

"Ms. Lizard just left this message for you." Mr. Rooster read the message to the Little Red Hen, "Nice seeing you today – taking your advice and heading to Bermuda for some fun – see you in a few months!"

He looked up from his notes to find a very shocked and silent Little Red Hen.

The Little Red Hen couldn't say anything – didn't want to say anything. She was embarrassed and frightened.

Thoughts began to race through her mind, "I pointed out how well the products would work, and how they would help them get the job done faster and more accurately, and that they would make their lives more secure. What was wrong with that?" she asked herself. "If that wasn't selling, then selling must be something very different from what I think it is," she thought.

Then she remembered a time long ago, when she needed to bake some bread and she had asked everyone she met if they would help... and no one would!

In a way, that was her first sales job and she had failed just as miserably. In fact, she ended up making the bread all alone. She had felt good about it that day, but how wrong she had been about feeling good. If she had only known, she never would have tried to be a salesperson.

She sank in the chair very depressed, "What a terrible salesperson I must be," she thought. "How could I have been so foolish to think I could sell." She felt like a drowned fowl slipping into the deep, dark ooze at the bottom of the pond. Her life must truly be over. She was going to end up just like Mr. Mule.

The Little Red Hen Learns Her Second Sales Lesson

"Little Red Hen," said Mr. Rooster gently, breaking the long silence in the room. "I need you to listen very carefully to see what I am about to say to you."

No response from the Little Red Hen.

Mr. Rooster continued, "Little Red Hen, after I finish sharing my observations with you, you will be ready for your next step in the journey of learning sales."

Still no response from the Little Red Hen.

"Little Red Hen. Look at me," commanded Mr. Rooster.

From far away, she heard his voice. As she heard her name again, she felt the blackness slip away, and she felt her body again. The Little Red Hen looked at Mr. Rooster with helplessness in her eyes.

"Yes," said the Little Red Hen in a meek voice. "I'm sorry. I guess I'm just not cut out for sales."

"On the contrary, Little Red Hen," said Mr. Rooster. "You have excellent qualities for sales: perseverance, dedication, hard work, a love of the product and what it will do for others. These qualities can help you become a great sales person – but only if you can learn to sell."

Mr. Rooster continued, "You have learned a great lesson – a lesson that could not be taught to you in class. You have learned that you do not understand selling."

"Are you ready for your next lesson?" asked Mr. Rooster.

Was she hearing correctly? Mr. Rooster was asking her if she was ready for her next lesson. What was her first lesson?

"Mr. Rooster, I don't understand," said the confused Little Red Hen. "What was my first lesson? And do I understand that you want me to keep working with you?"

"Absolutely, Little Red Hen," said Mr. Rooster. "Your first lesson was that you do not understand selling at all, and I think you have learned that lesson very well. Don't you agree?"

"Why, yes," said the Little Red Hen, still taken aback by his apparent excitement at her failure.

"First," continued Mr. Rooster, "many who have had an experience like this in sales will quit, never learning a most valuable communication lesson. The lesson is that *the majority of people who are in sales have no idea what sales is.* They believe it is making presentations and talking product and asking planned questions about placing orders."

"Isn't it?" asked the Little Red Hen.

"Well, didn't you do all those things?" replied Mr. Rooster.

"Yes."

"Did you get any sales?"

"No."

"Then would you say doing those things is effective selling?" asked Mr. Rooster.

"No, but all the other books talk about those things as being important," stressed the Little Red Hen.

"Yes, they are a part of selling. They are not the essence of selling. So let's set those books aside for a moment, Little Red Hen," said Mr. Rooster.

Mr. Rooster continued, "The first lesson in sales is to know that making presentations and talking product is not selling – it's talking!"

"Most people in sales positions spend their time talking not selling," said Mr. Rooster. "Which is why the people who apply technique to talking are never going to be successful in sales.

"The worst part is they don't even realize that they aren't selling when they think they're selling," said Mr. Rooster with genuine pain in his voice. "Little Red Hen," said Mr. Rooster, "can you tell me now what I just said to you? Can you tell me what the first lesson in selling is?"

"As I understand you," said the Little Red Hen, "the first lesson in selling is that selling is not talking product or making presentations, and that applying technique to talking is not going to help."

"And what about most people in sales?" asked Mr. Rooster.

"Most salespeople..." began the Little Red Hen.

"Not salespeople," Mr. Rooster interrupted. "Salespeople as I define them, know how they sell and when they sell. It's the others in sales that sell when they don't intend to and don't sell when they try to. Go on."

"Most people in sales don't know they aren't really selling. They don't even know when they are selling," said the Little Red Hen.

"So, what was <u>your</u> first lesson, Little Red Hen?" asked Mr. Rooster.

"I learned that I don't know how to sell or even when I am selling," said the Little Red Hen.

"Excellent!" shouted Mr. Rooster. "Now, what do you want to do? Do you want to continue selling, knowing that selling may be very different from what you think it is?"

"I understand why someone would quit right now," remarked the exhausted Little Red Hen.

"So do I. This is not a family for everyone," replied Mr. Rooster very gently.

"I feel all my friends must be right. That I can't learn," moaned the Little Red Hen.

"This has nothing to do with what anyone else thinks," said Mr. Rooster sternly. "This is something that is up to you and you alone. Do you want to quit?"

"No, I won't quit," said the Little Red Hen.

"Why?" asked Mr. Rooster.

"It's not just about selling the products. I have never felt I could get anyone to do anything for me. If I hadn't done it myself, I don't think anything would have been done," said the Little Red Hen. "That's how I've been successful so far in my life. But in this new world, I don't think just doing it myself will work. I need to be able to convince others to help me," reflected the Little Red Hen. "I'm sure the answer is out there – I just seem to be missing it."

Mr. Rooster smiled. "I'm glad you want to learn. At this moment, you are much closer than you think to finding the answer. In fact, this is the beginning of a whole new world for you, Little Red Hen," said Mr. Rooster encouragingly. "You need to go back to the barnyard, because you're right, the answer is right there in front of you," said Mr. Rooster. "Everyone has been selling all along – including you. You just haven't noticed what goes on when you are selling."

"I would like you to come back next Tuesday afternoon and we will discuss what you are observing and learning," said Mr. Rooster.

The Little Red Hen looked at him in confusion. "The answer is in my very own barnyard?"

"Yes, it is," said Mr. Rooster. "What I want you to do in the barnyard is stop seeing the world from your perspective and see it from everyone else's perspective! Once you do that you will have all the security you need, and you will belong to the family of sales." And with that he wished her luck and sent her on her way.

"But where do I start?" asked the still confused Little Red Hen.

"That is what you should think about and try to figure out," said Mr. Rooster. "Until next Tuesday, Little Red Hen."

The Little Red Hen
Explores the Barnyard

Returning to the barnyard, the confused Little Red Hen did not have the faintest clue what good this would do. She knew every inch of this place. She knew the other animals, and she knew their habits. She knew what they liked and didn't like; who was nice, and who was grumpy.

Still, Mr. Rooster must know something she didn't, because she had just learned that she knew nothing about selling, and there must be some reason he sent her here. So she sat down and watched. She didn't really want to talk to anyone anyway, not after her failure. They had all said she would fail. Despite the nice words Mr. Rooster had said for encouragement, she still felt like a complete failure. So she would just stay to the side and observe.

She searched all day for the answer. Nothing. Her head hurt from trying to hear what everyone was saying, and her eyes were tired from trying to see something different and find some answer.

No matter how hard she tried, as the sun slowly set behind the golden hills, everything looked the same to the Little Red Hen. Disappointed, she headed home as the first stars appeared in the evening sky.

The Little Red Hen Hears the Train

After making a light supper, the exhausted Little Red Hen dragged herself to bed. She was too tired to concentrate on learning sales, and too tired to fall asleep. So she let her thoughts drift without effort.

All day the Little Red Hen had listened and looked for the answer Mr. Rooster had said was in the barnyard. Questions kept running through her head. "What am I missing? Could I have focused harder? Mr. Rooster had said it was in the barnyard, so it must be here someplace."

All these thoughts and questions were like having a marching band in her head. With no answers coming, the thoughts just piled up and made her tense. She was never going to find sleep this way.

The Little Red Hen took some deep breaths, cleared her mind, and let her tension slip away. As she did, a strange thing happened. She began to notice things around her. She felt her head on the pillow. She saw the soft glow from the moonlight shining in her room. She heard the breeze glide under the door. She heard the leaves rustle on the branches...and far off she heard the train.

She hadn't heard the train for years, not because it had stopped coming by, but because she had become accustomed to it. She realized it went by every night. She had become accustomed to it going by and didn't consciously hear it. She immediately jumped out of bed.

"What if everything in the barnyard looked the same because I have become accustomed to it?" she said out loud as she paced the floor. What if she was missing things, a great many things, because they were overlooked through familiarity?

She knew immediately that she was indeed overlooking many things. She suspected that some of those things were very important to understanding others and communicating clearly.

How did this happen? How did everything become so invisible to her!

When she was a little chick, she worked hard to see everything and do everything. Every day was a new experience and the experience was to learn. There was so much to think about growing up.

For the most part now, she did the majority of her activities without thinking. Just like the farmer's son when he learned to drive the tractor. At first, he had trouble remembering which lever to push and what the right time was to push it. Now, he did it all without thinking, and he could do many other things at the same time.

This thought gave her a sense of security. "If the farmer's son can do it, so can I," thought the Little Red Hen. So she lay back down in bed.

She knew that she could learn something, practice it until she mastered it, and eventually do it without thinking about it. She wondered what else she heard without really listening.

Familiarity makes sounds silent and objects invisible. Mr. Rooster was right, of course. The answer was right in front of her and had been all day long. The answer to sales was not about hearing, but about listening, and not about watching, but about seeing.

A big yawn escaped from the Little Red Hen as she wondered, "What else is so familiar to me that I am no longer aware of it?"

The Little Red Hen fell fast asleep.

The Little Red Hen Learns about Agreement

The next day was a bright and sunshiny day. It was a brand new day in a brand new life for the Little Red Hen – everything was new and alive. The Little Red Hen was completely relaxed. A great weight had been lifted from her shoulders. She watched and she listened to everything anew.

As she headed out the door of her cozy home to the barnyard, she saw the hairline crack in the flowerpot on her windowsill.

As she walked down the path, she saw the sun's rays shine on the dewdrops, dancing with the spider's web. She saw little rainbows in the dewdrops.

As she past the last row of trees before the barnyard, she heard the leaves rustle with the morning breeze.

Once in the barnyard, she noticed that it looked different – more alive than ever. She didn't want to interfere with it, and since she wanted to watch without being interrupted, she found a secure spot close enough to hear everything, yet out of sight from everyone, on a perch in the hayloft of the barn. It was one of the places she would hide when she played as a little chick. Hidden from view, she sat down and waited and watched with the veil of familiarity removed.

She saw Mr. Rooster make his rounds and noticed he sometimes stopped and talked and sometimes he didn't.

She listened to his conversations, "Hello, Mr. Frog. Great day, isn't it?"

Mr. Frog replied, "Yes, it certainly is!"

Mr. Rooster stopped and talked before moving on.

"Hello, Mr. Mule," said Mr. Rooster, "Nice day, isn't it?"

"Yes, but it probably won't last," replied Mr. Mule.

Mr. Rooster walked on without a moment's hesitation.

"Great day, Mr. Skunk," said Mr. Rooster.

"Yes, and I heard a storm is coming," responded Mr. Skunk.

Mr. Rooster stopped to talk.

After they finished talking, Mr. Rooster looked directly at the Little Red Hen and smiled. Then he walked on.

The Little Red Hen was dumbfounded. "Did he know I was here? If Mr. Rooster did, he must know things that I am only beginning to discover," thought the Little Red Hen.

The Little Red Hen thought to herself, "Three opportunities to talk and Mr. Rooster only stopped for two. What was the difference? One agreed it was a great day. One agreed and said a storm was coming. One agreed, but said it wouldn't last. So, it couldn't have been agreement with Mr. Rooster's greeting. Mr. Skunk actually thought a storm was coming, which will make it not such a great day.

"Maybe it was how the comment was presented. Maybe it was the words they chose.

"Two said *and*... one said *but*. Mr. Mule said *but*, and that's the one Mr. Rooster didn't stop for. Maybe he thought it would have been a negative conversation. Did the word *but* trigger that?"

Before today, she would not have even noticed word use during a conversation, especially such a small difference as using *and* or *but*. Today was different. Today she noticed everything. She decided to listen to those two words being used in the barnyard all day.

She listened to many conversations throughout the day.

At the end of the day, a tired and happy Little Red Hen began her journey home. She smiled as she walked down the path, because she had discovered something that had been right in front of her all along: Almost every time someone said *but* instead of *and*, it seemed to set up some level of discord. Depending on the topic, the tone, and the situation, the one thing that remained consistent was if someone was trying to sell someone on something, it made a big difference whether they used the words *and* or *but*.

In fact, she had heard almost identical statements from the Weasel twins talking to their mother except for one word. Tommy Weasel said, "I will get my work done *and* I want to play." Billy Weasel said, "I will get my work done, *but* I want to play." Billy got sent back to work with a cuff on the cheek, while Tommy got to play a few minutes before having to finish his work.

"Could one word make that much difference? It seemed it did," thought the Little Red Hen.

She thought back to her sales appointment with Mr. Horse. She could vaguely remember saying *but* to him.

'Did I say *but*?" she wondered. "If I did, how could I change that?"

So, as the sun set beyond the farm, and the tired and happy Little Red Hen walked down the path, she reviewed what she had learned. Using the word *and...* instead of *but...* could greatly help develop a position of agreement. In fact, disagreement in ideas was better received if the transition from one idea to another was done with *and*.

The Little Red Hen thought about the majority of those in sales. She wondered if they were so interested in showing their knowledge that they would want to correct those with whom they were talking. Maybe that was one of the problems with talking. The Little Red Hen knew this was a very important concept.

"Can I change my use of words?" she asked herself.

What if she did say *but* out of habit? How would she change to using *and*? This might be one of those easy-to-understand concepts that was actually hard to implement.

"I am not sure, *but...* oops," thought the Little Red Hen. "I am not sure, *and* if I catch myself every time I say *but* and practice using *and* by repeating my talk or thought, I should eventually be able to eliminate, or at least reduce, the habit of saying *but*," thought the Little Red Hen.

"I will do this! This will be my perfect practice," said the Little Red Hen.

She knew this practice was the answer! The way to get rid of one habit was to practice the desired habit over and over again. She would catch herself every time she said *but*, and repeat what she had said using *and*. Not only that, she would ask others to catch her as well so they could help her become very aware of when she said *but*. She would then replace it with *and*.

The Little Red Hen carried these thoughts with her and practiced all the way home. She practiced while she had dinner. She practiced while she got herself ready for bed. She practiced for a short time in her cozy bed.

It was a very short time, because soon the tired Little Red Hen was fast asleep.

The Little Red Hen Learns about Personalities

On Sunday, the Little Red Hen awakened to the sound of her fax machine spitting out a piece of paper. It was a fax from Mr. Rooster.

Little Red Hen,

There are four critters that you are likely to find down by the pond if you looked around: Wasps, ants, butterflies, and pollywogs. As you picture these critters, I'd like you to think of them as representing the four basic approaches to decision-making personalities.

The wasps, which get right down to business when they have something to accomplish, are your bottom-line and to-the-point decision-makers.

The ants, which are organized and logical, are your linear, step-by-step, lots-of-details decision-makers.

The butterflies, which float from flower to flower, are your socially oriented decision-makers, spending more time finding out what others think and how they feel before making a decision.

The pollywogs, which speed from one direction to another, are your fun and excited decision-makers, looking forward to change and something new.

Think back to your four sales appointments. What were the decision-making styles of your prospects? And knowing that, what would you do differently? And finally, if you are able to use this information, Little Red Hen, do you think it will give you a greater sense of security and make you feel a part of the family of selling?

Sincerely,

Mr. Rooster

P.S. Questions are so important to discovery – don't you agree, Little Red Hen?

"Yes," thought the Little Red Hen, "questions are very important." She had been noticing that through the use of questions she had been guided by Ms. Peacock to call on Mr. Rooster. Questions were how Mr. Rooster had kept her working on selling and how he was now helping her. The Little Red Hen was discovering just how important questions were. Not only did they uncover information, they put her in a position to talk less.

The Little Red Hen thought about Mr. Rooster's first question and her sales calls. What were the decision-making styles of her prospects?

It immediately became clear to her that they each represented one of the four personalities.

Mr. Horse was a wasp. He was bottom-lined and to the point. As soon as he made up his mind, the sales call was over. It was not too much detail that was the problem for Mr. Horse. It was that she did not focus in on his bottomline.

Ms. Pig was a butterfly. She was interested in chatting and visiting, building the relationship. Here, the Little Red Hen was so focused on the presentation, she didn't visit at all. And Ms. Hog was a relationship of hers, someone who needed Ms. Pig.

Mr. Duck was the ant. Exacting, detailed, and regimented. Being late set things off to a bad start. If she had called him, he would not have thought badly about her, he would have thought she was being meticulous and thorough. His exacting time allocation for the meeting was a clue she was given in the fax before she had even begun talking to him.

Ms. Lizard was the pollywog. She was going off in a million different directions. She loved the excitement and fun of doing something new.

"Oh my!" thought the Little Red Hen. "I had indeed sold her something! I sold Ms. Lizard on going to Bermuda!"

The Little Red Hen plopped down feeling very dizzy. Mr. Rooster's words rung hard in her head:

"The average salesperson does not even know when they are selling."

This was an entirely different world. In fact, she was a little frightened. If she had missed these things, which were so obvious, what else was she missing?

After she had composed herself a little, she thought, "I wonder if I could use this in the barnyard?"

She thought about her discovery yesterday of the important difference between *and* and *but* and her commitment to practice.

"Oh, yes I can, and I can practice with everyone I meet," decided the Little Red Hen. "In fact," continued the Little Red Hen, "I wonder if I have noticed this before and just not realized its importance." She thought about others in the barnyard she knew.

Ms. Beaver was also an ant. She was detailed and meticulous. Ms. Squirrel was a pollywog, running around finding new nuts and running back to her nest all excited. Ms. Peacock was a butterfly and she related to people, which may have been why Little Red Hen went to see her first. And Mr. Rooster was a wasp, just like the Little Red Hen. Mr. Rooster, however, knew he was a wasp. He also knew that he had to pay attention to the personality approaches of others, while she only operated in her approach.

She thought back to making the bread long ago. Her approach had been, I'm going to get this done and you can help me or not – a very wasp-like approach. What if she had approached people more to their style of decision-making?

"I know it would have made a significant difference," thought the Little Red Hen.

Maybe this was an answer to understanding the essence of selling. It wasn't having the perfect product knowledge or all the answers or the price they expected. It was approaching people in different styles – their style.

"Approaching people with their communication style lets them know that you understand them," thought the Little Red Hen. "It demonstrates to them verbally and visually that you are interested in communicating with them."

She knew now that she had to practice both communicating with agreement by using *and* verses *but* and communicating to others in their personality style.

"I know that I am on the road to sales success, and I know there is so much more to learn," thought the Little Red Hen.

And of course she was right.

She headed to the barnyard to practice her skills and see what else she could learn. After all, she had a couple more days before she saw Mr. Rooster again.

On her way to the barnyard, she thought specifically about the fax from Mr. Rooster. There was something more in it than just the description of the personalities, something even more important. It seemed tied to her desire to act on the information about the descriptions. She could not nail it down, *but ...*

... *and* it must be something very important.

The Little Red Hen Practices in the Barnyard

All day long, the Little Red Hen watched others communicating. She saw how agreement was maintained with *and* statements. While she noticed *and* did not solve all differences or stop all communication problems, it made an enormous difference to the potential for success. *And* worked best when it was as much a part of attitude as it was the verbiage. Maybe that was the key, saying and communicating ways to work together versus being separate.

She saw the magic of communication when one adapted their style and spoke with others in an approach in which the other felt comfortable. When Billy Weasel wanted to cross over the dam Ms. Beaver built, he stood taller and asked rather formally, "Ms. Beaver, may I cross from this side to the other and later back again just today for efficiency and fun. I weigh only one pound and will step carefully in the places you designate."

"Of course," said Ms. Beaver.

When brother Tommy Weasel tried to follow without asking, he was stopped short.

"Where do you think you are going?" demanded Ms. Beaver.

"I just wanted to cut across. Come on, it'll only take a second," pleaded Tommy Weasel.

"No, that is not OK," affirmed Ms. Beaver. "And it's not just a second. It's the principle of it. You didn't care enough to ask."

The Little Red Hen noticed how the approach in dealing with someone was as important as what was talked about. She noticed that some were good at matching another's personality approach and others weren't. She suspected that a few knew what they were doing, but most didn't.

"Ah-ha... a few knew what they were doing, and most didn't. That phrase has a familiar ring to it," thought the Little Red Hen.

She watched the Weasel brothers further.

Billy Weasel asked several more times to cross Ms. Beaver's bridge. She let him over one more time. The next few requests by Billy met with a refusal by Ms. Beaver. In fact, the last time he asked, in much the same way he had asked before, she told him not to ask anymore.

"May I cross again, Ms. Beaver, so that I can repeat precisely my previous journey for efficiency and fun?" asked Billy.

"Billy, you are as bad as your brother. You are more focused on fun than efficiency!" explained Ms. Beaver. "And you're interfering with my efficiency. Now go away and don't ask again!"

"Wow!" thought the Little Red Hen. 'There must be something else in his communication that nullified his matching her personality style, because communicating with agreement and matching personality did not guarantee the result. I wonder what it is?"

The Little Red Hen tried hard to come up with the answer. Try as she might, it didn't come to her at that moment.

The Little Red Hen Learns about Cups and Corn

As the day wore on, the Little Red Hen grew tired. The harder she tried to focus, the harder it was to stay focused. Eventually, she just relaxed.

She let her eyes close and listened. She was surprised to find it already becoming easier to hear agreement and recognize personalities. These new skills were becoming second nature for her.

The security she found in her new skills, along with her fatigue, soon led the Little Red Hen's mind to wandering. As she drifted into a dreamlike state, she heard a mother hen scolding her chicks.

"Don't eat these seeds," scolded the mother hen. "They're poisonous!"

"That's nice," thought the dreamy Little Red Hen. "Why would the mother be so upset? Poisonous seeds did not kill the chicks, they just wouldn't grow to be as strong as those who didn't eat them, and they knew that. Some ate the seeds anyway."

The Little Red Hen became very awake. "Why would the chicks eat seeds that were not good for them when they knew better?"

Everyone knew that the chicks who ate the seeds that were good for them were the strongest. Chicks that ate the seeds from poisonous plants were smaller and weaker.

"Why would the chicks do that?" thought the Little Red Hen again.

Then the Little Red Hen had a series of thoughts that seemed strange to her. It was as if Mr. Rooster was speaking in her head.

"Chicks make decisions – all kinds of decisions – everyone does. They decide what to eat – be it healthy or unhealthy. They decide where to play – be it safe or unsafe. They decide with whom to talk – be they of good nature or bad nature. They decide when to work hard and when to relax."

She saw in her mind little cups of seeds, good seeds and poisonous seeds; and little cups of places to play, safe and unsafe; and little cups of people to spend time with, people of good nature and bad nature. She saw in her mind the chicks choosing from each of the cups. She realized that it was a choice for the chicks to do or not do something. Just like in sales.

Someone could buy or not buy – it was a choice.

Her focus was brought back to the barnyard by laughing. She looked at the chicks and found mother hen gone and the chicks daring each other to eat the poisonous seeds. Some took the dare and ate the poisonous seeds.

The Little Red Hen thought to herself, "Why would they take that dare? They knew those seeds could make them sick. They knew that they could get into trouble. So why do it?" she thought. "Unless, they get something else from doing it!" thought the Little Red Hen, turning around because it was as if Mr. Rooster had just tapped her on the shoulder.

"Why yes, that's it!" she surprised herself by talking out loud. "They must get other things from their choices!" she realized.

"But what were they?" she thought and then she caught the *but* in her thought process. "*And* what were they?" she rephrased. "This perfect practice thing takes a great deal of effort," she mused.

The Little Red Hen did not know what else they got from their choices, and she guessed it to be something that came from inside them. "Maybe it was a belief, a feeling, a vision of themselves about taking a risk, accepting a challenge or facing a dare," thought the Little Red Hen.

The Little Red Hen knew that the food people ate nourished them. She knew that depending upon what they ate, they would be happy and healthy or sick and miserable.

Now, she began to think of every decision as a choice of feeding themselves and keeping them healthy. While food related to someone's physical health, other choices related to mental health and happiness. It was as if someone had internal cups that needed to be filled.

Then she developed three very clear thoughts in the form of questions:

What makes someone choose to do something even when it might look to everyone else to be bad for them?

What defined these mental cups for individuals?

What is it that fills these internal cups and makes individuals happy?

She laughed to herself when she realized that she was thinking in questions.

She knew these were very important questions to discover, and it was a good time to go home and go to bed. So she did just that.

The Little Red Hen
Learns about Filling Cups

When she awoke in the morning, her first thoughts were about the three questions.

What makes someone choose to do something even when it might be bad for them?

What defined these mental cups for individuals?

What is it that fills these internal cups and makes individuals happy?

Seeds and water contributed to physical health. Seeds and water had value. The Little Red Hen started off by considering things as good or bad. For example, she thought you could define some seeds as having good value and others as having bad value, or some water as having good value and other water as having bad value, but that distinction wouldn't hold true. What was not good for someone might be good for another. The chicks couldn't drink the swamp water without getting sick, and Mr. Frog couldn't live without it. So, the water had value and it was different to different creatures.

"Ah-ha," thought the Little Red Hen.

So maybe there were things that contributed to the mental health of people that were like seeds and water – not good or bad, just different. Not wanting to waste too much time defining them, she decided to refer to these things that contributed to mental health – that filled people's cups – as values. She thought about how when the food cups were empty the chicks wanted their food cups filled. In the same way, the Little Red Hen bet that the chicks wanted their mental value cups filled as well.

The Little Red Hen decided her afternoon would be spent watching the chicks in the barnyard.

The Little Red Hen
Learns about Decision-Making

Once she arrived in the barnyard, the Little Red Hen saw a chick looking at two pieces of corn on the ground. The pieces of corn were the same size, color, and shape, identical in every way. The chick looked at both and then picked the one on the right.

The Little Red Hen, who had learned the importance of questions, stopped and asked the little chick, "Why did you pick the one on the right?"

The little chick replied, "Because mother hen said that if I picked right first whenever I could, I'd find comfort." Then the little chick gobbled up the corn left on the ground and moved along.

The Little Red Hen thought about what the little chick said. She thought about the *which* question... *which* one did he pick... he picked the one on the right. But if the little chick had been coming from the other direction, the other one would have been on the right. So the *which* question didn't help in this case – and it didn't matter if the chick's logic was flawed because it was his belief that was important.

It was the *why* and *what* questions that led the Little Red Hen to the answer.

Why did he pick the one on his right? His mom told him to pick the one on the right.

And *what would he get from picking that one:* comfort.

So with everything the same: the little chick took the one that would feed his mind with comfort.

"The little chick's internal cup, his value, is comfort," said the Little Red Hen to herself. "It's like an internal measuring cup, a judge and jury, that lets the chick know he is making the right decision," reasoned the Little Red Hen.

"I must check this out further tomorrow," thought the Little Red Hen. "Today, I'm going home early and get a good night's sleep."

When she arrived at home, she found a package and a note from Mr. Rooster. The note read:

My guess is that you are learning a great deal about your new world. I think it would add to your security of knowledge by capturing your discoveries. Don't you agree, Little Red Hen? In a way, it is like a family album of ideas.

The Little Red Hen opened the box to find a leather bound journal with her name embossed on the cover.

The Little Red Hen wrote down her discoveries of that day regarding values. She knew there would be much more to write about tomorrow.

She was right, of course.

She was soon tucked under the covers and had a very good night's sleep.

The Little Red Hen Practices with Values

At the barnyard the next morning, the Little Red Hen placed herself in front of the chick she had talked to yesterday as he was pecking his way through the barnyard. The Little Red Hen held out two kernels of corn before him.

"These kernels are special," said the Little Red Hen. "This one gives comfort and this one gives power. "You can only have one," said the Little Red Hen. "Which one do you want?"

"Oh, I want the one that gives comfort," said the little chick.

"Umm," said the Little Red Hen. "That's a good choice. And the one that gives comfort will cost you three kernels of regular corn."

"Oh," said the little chick, "how much does the other one cost?"

"I will tell you in a moment," said the Little Red Hen. "If you will answer a question for me. Why did you ask about the price of the other one?"

"Because I get comfort when I save my money, and I only spend it on important things."

"Fair enough," said the Little Red Hen. "The kernel that gives power is only two kernels of regular corn so it is less expensive."

The little chick only hesitated for a moment. "Yes, I would like the kernel of corn that gives comfort for three kernels of corn."

"But that is more expensive than the one that gives you power," said the Little Red Hen.

"Yes, it is, but I don't need power," replied the little chick.

"Ah-ha," thought the Little Red Hen to herself. "What if it only cost one kernel?" asked the Little Red Hen.

"Oh, why then I would take it," stated the little chick, "because I would have so much comfort from saving two kernels of corn that I would feel very comfortable."

"Thank you," said the Little Red Hen. "You may have them both for free."

"Thank you, but I insist on paying for the one that provides comfort, if it's worth having it at all," said the little chick.

"It is worth the three kernels and it's not for free," apologized the Little Red Hen, recognizing that her word choice was negatively affecting the decision-making process. "They are my gift to you, because you have earned them by taking your time to answer my questions."

"Thank you," said the little chick, who took the kernels offered and headed off to find mother hen.

After the little chick left, the Little Red Hen wrote her observations in her journal. The little chick was willing to spend more money for something associated with comfort, something that would give him comfort.

"So, values drive decisions and money is a thing that is associated with a value," thought the Little Red Hen. Was this what had been happening with Mr. Horse? Did she, in some way, not address his values in association with pricing?

The Little Red Hen sat down. Her head was spinning again from these new discoveries. She knew she was just beginning to really understand how little she knew about selling.

Late in the day, the little chick sought out the Little Red Hen. This time the little chick had friends with him. "Do you have some more special kernels?" asked the little chicks.

Not wishing to start something that would be bad for the chick colony, everyone thinking she had magic seeds, the Little Red Hen said, "No, I do not."

The Little Red Hen was curious to know more about how the little chick made decisions so she used a *What if* question. "If I did have some kernels that would give comfort and some that give power, which would you want?"

"Oh, the ones that give comfort," said the little chick she had talked to earlier.

"Even at twice the price?" said the Little Red Hen.

"Yes, yes," said the little chick.

"No," said the smallest of the little chick's friends.

"Is it too expensive?" the Little Red Hen asked the smallest chick.

"Who cares about the cost?" said the smallest chick. "I want the one that gives power."

"No," said the biggest chick in the brood. "Why give up the security of money for either?"

"Yes," said the last remaining chick. "I will get comfort from the power I gain and the security of saving money!"

The little band of chicks took to arguing with one another as the Little Red Hen walked away. In her journal she wrote, "Chicks have different values and they associate values differently with actions, things, and decisions."

This was excellent information. Now how could she use it? She sat and thought of questions that would help her.

"What are the values of those I deal with?" was a question the Little Red Hen thought valuable. This led to another good question, "How do you find out the values of others?"

The Little Red Hen was concentrating so hard on other questions related to that thought, that she almost missed the very interesting conversation going on nearby. Quickly the Little Red Hen jotted down in her journal: "Need to have questions ready so you can listen effectively."

"That was certainly an ah-ha!" she thought as she turned her full attention to the nearby conversation.

"So what are you going to do for vacation?" asked the brown hen to the fluffy hen.

The fluffy hen replied, "We're going to stay at the old window lying in the marsh. You know, the one that came down the river in the flood."

"Oh, why would you go there?" said the brown hen.

"Why it's the perfect place to relax," said the fluffy hen. "The days are warm with the sun shining through the glass, there's plenty to eat and there's lots of down to curl up in at night to stay warm…."

The Little Red Hen almost jumped up with excitement.

"That's it!" she shouted. "That's the answer."

"All you have to do is ask them why they made that decision, and they will choose the words that define their values!" thought the Little Red Hen.

She was so excited she decided to call it a day and get to bed early. So she hurried to her nice secure home.

Tomorrow was her last day before seeing Mr. Rooster. She wondered what new discovery she would find. She knew now that learning sales was a life long journey – and she was only beginning.

Feeling very happy with herself, the Little Red Hen had dinner and went to bed.

She slept very soundly.

The Little Red Hen Discovers Framing

The Little Red Hen noticed that the little chick she watched for the past two days was now hanging around with a different group of friends. She listened to their conversation.

"After that big argument about what was important," said the little chick to his new friends, "I just realized that I looked at the world differently from the other chicks. And for right now that's not a comfortable position for me."

She listened for a while to the little chick talk and heard him mention comfort a lot:

"I can't see myself comfortable any more."

"I need to hear the comfort of your voice."

"It's not comfortable when you realize you think differently from those around you."

She heard his new friends respond in kind:

"We feel very comfortable with you."

"I see you able to fit in very easily here."

"I hear what you're saying."

Sounded to the Little Red Hen like the little chick's comfort cup was very empty. The Little Red Hen knew that once his comfort cup was filled the chick eventually would get back together with his old friends.

What fascinated her was that they were using different sensing words to describe their comfort: see, hear, and feel.

She thought maybe they were operating with different sensory perceptions.

"Did the sensing words used to relate to another make a difference in the conversation?" thought the Little Red Hen. After listening, she felt it did. She decided to call the three different sensory areas "frames". They were a visual frame, auditory frame, and kinesthetic frame.

She noticed those that operated in a visual frame used visual words like see, picture, and look. While those in an auditory frame used sound words like hear, sound, and listen. Kinesthetic framed individuals used feel words like touch, contact, grip, and feel.

She noticed that difficulties arose when someone cross-framed, as she called it, when they replied to a visual frame with an auditory frame.

She noticed that cross-framing lead to blank looks and arguments.

While she was listening for framing, she lost track of *ands* and *buts* and values.

"There's so much to listen to!" she cried out loud. "Wow!"

"There were different personality approaches, different values, and different frames to listen for. This could be quite tiring." She could see how those in sales could miss so much if they did not have this understanding.

She had heard about listening harder, but she didn't know what that meant. Now she knew. Listening harder meant she had more listening to do. She had agreement to listen for, and personalities, and values, and now framing.

"Wow, it will take a lot of practice to get very good at listening to so much," thought the Little Red Hen. "And I will do it for my own security," she decided as she linked her own values to the task at hand.

The Little Red Hen Returns to Mr. Rooster

The next morning, the Little Red Hen could hardly wait to get in to see Mr. Rooster. She was so excited about her discoveries and so grateful to Mr. Rooster.

First, she thanked him for the journal and showed him how much she'd written.

She told him about the importance of maintaining agreement and how using *and...* instead of *but...* could make a huge difference.

She told him about the all the personalities she had observed after he had sent her the information on the four major personalities for making decisions.

She told him about values and how they seemed to be the key to decision-making.

Finally, she told him about frames, and how they would forever change the way she communicated with others.

Mr. Rooster was pleased with the Little Red Hen.

"Have you been practicing your newly discovered skills Little Red Hen?" he asked.

"Yes," replied the Little Red Hen, "I've been practicing each day. I practice in the barnyard and in my home. I practice on the road when I talk to others – even if it's only for a few minutes. How else will I become a master like you?!"

"You have learned well, Little Red Hen," said Mr. Rooster. "And now it's time for you to put your new-found skills to the test. I would like you to follow-up with Mr. Horse, Ms. Pig, Mr. Duck, and Ms. Lizard. See how they are doing and try out your skills. Do you think you can do that?" asked Mr. Rooster.

"Yes, that would be perfect," said the Little Red Hen.

"Good. Mr. Horse happened to call today and said he would be in his office at 10 o'clock. You can see him then," finished Mr. Rooster.

And as she was leaving with a smile, Mr. Rooster stopped her to ask one final question. "Little Red Hen."

"Yes?"

"On your way, could you think of how Ms. Peacock sold you on coming to see me? I'm sure she touched on your values. What do you think?"

Although she was caught a little off guard at the thought, the Little Red Hen realized that indeed she had been sold on pursuing her dream by coming to see Mr. Rooster. "Yes, I will, and thank you, Mr. Rooster."

"My pleasure, Little Red Hen."

And with that, the Little Red Hen left to see Mr. Horse. She realized how grateful she was to Mr. Rooster and Ms. Peacock for helping her sell herself on her success.

The Little Red Hen Makes It Happen

Ms. Pig was right on the way to the corral, so the Little Red Hen thought she'd take her chances by dropping in. This would leave her plenty of time to get to Mr. Horse's by 10 o'clock.

As the Little Red Hen walked down the path, she thought about Ms. Peacock. What were the words Ms. Peacock had said to her that day? First, Ms. Peacock had listened more than talked. She had asked questions. She had used *and* in her statements. It was all coming back now.

Ms. Peacock had used the words security and family. They were both important values to the Little Red Hen. The Little Red Hen was amazed at how quickly Ms. Peacock had picked up on her values.

"Should she really be amazed?" thought the Little Red Hen. "Didn't everyone share their values with every decision made? Hadn't she been sharing values with everyone in the barnyard her whole life? Of course she had. Everyone did, because they wanted their cups filled. All someone had to do was take the time to listen – just like she did in the barnyard with the chicks."

As the Little Red Hen approached Ms. Pig's place, she knew she had a great deal of work ahead of her. She had missed her first opportunity to establish a relationship with Ms. Pig, and Ms. Pig had solidified her existing relationship with her friend, Ms. Hog. This call would put all her new skills to the test.

Ms. Pig was quite surprised to see the Little Red Hen walking down the path to her pigpen. When it became obvious to her that the Little Red Hen was going to stop, Ms. Pig met her at the gate. Ms. Pig kept the gate closed.

"Hello, Ms. Pig," said the Little Red Hen, noticing that Ms. Pig was keeping the gate between them. "I just wanted to drop in and say hello. I was so focused last time about providing information that I didn't take any time to get to know you."

"I understand how that is," replied Ms. Pig, "and I would love to spend time with you, but I have so much to do right now."

The Little Red Hen took notice of the *but* in Ms. Pig's response. "Yes, I can see that," said the Little Red Hen, "and how do you keep your place so beautiful?"

"It does take a lot of effort, but it's a labor of love," expressed Ms. Pig, not relaxing her position behind the gate.

"I'll bet your family and friends enjoy it," continued the Little Red Hen.

"Yes, they do," said Ms. Pig.

"Speaking of friends, you mentioned Ms. Hog the last time I was here," said the Little Red Hen. "Mr. Rooster spoke very highly of her."

"Yes, she is a very good friend," said Ms. Pig.

"Mr. Rooster tells me that she has a product that is similar to the one we talked about," said the Little Red Hen. "He said they are both very good products and could each do the job for you. He also said we have a family of products that will support either product really well," said the Little Red

Hen as she turned to go. "Well, I won't keep you. Should I call sometime so that we can get together for lunch?"

Ms. Pig was a little surprised by her own response as she stepped out from behind the gate. "Why, yes, of course, Little Red Hen. How about later this week?"

And so the Little Red Hen ended up staying a little while longer as they made plans to visit.

Once on her way again to the corral to see Mr. Horse, she came across Mr. Duck entering the path in the direction she was walking.

"Well, hello, Mr. Duck," initiated the Little Red Hen without slowing down. "What do you surmise the temperature to be right now?"

"It's 88.75 degrees, Little Red Hen," said Mr. Duck. "Just below the yearly average for this month."

"Is this year a little cooler than most?" inquired the Little Red Hen.

"By my calculations, it is. Keeping track of temperatures is a little hobby of mine," responded Mr. Duck.

"Really, and what do you enjoy most about your hobby?" asked the Little Red Hen.

"I get a peace of mind in rediscovering the weather patterns each year." acknowledged Mr. Duck as he motioned to the Little Red Hen that he was turning to a different path.

"Well, it looks as if we part ways for the moment," said the Little Red Hen. "I'd really enjoy more details on your calculations sometime in the future. And maybe I could go over some of the products in greater detail in which you have interest so you'd have the same peace of mind when you make your decision about them. Should I call your office to schedule an appointment?"

"Yes, please do," said Mr. Duck as he smiled before hurrying on his way.

The Little Red Hen was amazed at this new world. She learned in a few minutes' conversation some important values of Ms. Pig (family) and Mr. Duck (peace of mind). How could she have missed this before? It seemed so easy to comprehend.

Then a most amazing thing happened. The Little Red Hen realized why she baked the bread so long ago: it gave her a sense of security to be independent and it allowed her to provide for her family. No wonder she was so pleased with herself on that day.

It was also a loss of that security and the possible loss of her home with the arrival of that letter that made her day so depressing before she decided to call on Ms. Peacock about selling houses.

Right then and there, the Little Red Hen made a commitment to herself to do things to fill her cups each and every day.

As the corral came into view, she switched her focus to Mr. Horse. "How did the conversation go before?", thought the Little Red Hen, not able to recall the exact words used by either of them. "Maybe I'll get lucky and get a second chance to uncover his values," thought the Little Red Hen. This was her final thought before entering the corral. She had learned from watching in the barnyard, if you wanted to be effective, your entire focus had to be on others.

To put it mildly, Mr. Horse was not thrilled to see the Little Red Hen coming up the path to the corral. He had expected Mr. Rooster.

"Hello, Mr. Horse," opened the Little Red Hen. "I am here at Mr. Rooster's request to make sure that everything is in order with your purchase."

"I had expected to see Mr. Rooster himself," said Mr. Horse, getting right to the point. "He seems to understand my needs very well. I'm not sure that we can accomplish what I need without him."

The Little Red Hen smiled as she heard this. She thought, "How very lucky I am to be in a different world."

"Yes, he does understand your needs very well," confirmed the Little Red Hen, "and the importance of accomplishing what was intended to be accomplished, which is why I am here. To properly finish what I improperly started."

"Well then," replied Mr. Horse. "Let's get on with it."

And after a very short time, staying very focused and to the point, Mr. Horse had ordered a host of products to help him accomplish to a greater degree what he wanted. He thanked the Little Red Hen and made an appointment for her to follow-up with him next week.

The Little Red Hen was very pleased. She left Mr. Horse's, not just with an order, she left with a greater sense of security than she had ever had in her life. She realized that Ms.

Peacock and Mr. Rooster had introduced her to a new world and she was now part of the greatest family in the world – the family of sales.

She realized that she was extremely happy. And why shouldn't she be? Her two most important cups were filled – security and family. Two great salespeople had made sure of that – Ms. Peacock and Mr. Rooster.

As she walked home, she noticed the cool breeze, the gently swaying flowers, and the buzzing bees moving from flower to flower. Today was perfect.

"I need to thank Mr. Rooster and Ms. Peacock," thought the Little Red Hen. "Of course, I'll make them each a loaf of bread." and with that thought she smiled even bigger.

She could hardly wait until Ms. Lizard returned from Bermuda for the fun to really begin.

In the meantime, maybe she'd pay a visit to Ms. Peacock to deliver some bread and thank her for her help. They might end up talking about the Little Red Hen selling houses or possibly buying another one – just for the security of the investment, of course.

The End

About the Author

Jeffrey Hansler has been in sales since he was 9 years old selling candy door-to-door for his football uniform. He says he finally learned the art of sales 21 years later. He describes his success up until that time as a combination of hard work and luck.

Since becoming a full time speaker and educator in 1992 the list of clients he has provided training for is extensive and includes many industries and market leaders: Associations, Aerospace, Automotive, Colleges/Universities, Document Management, Financial, Government, Healthcare, High Tech, Manufacturing, Wholesale, Non-Profit, Real Estate, Property Management, Retail, Service, Telecommunications, Transportation, Theme Parks. Companies include Aetna, AGFA Bayer, Allied Van Lines, AT&T, AT&T Wireless, Atlas Travel, Boeing Corporation, Borg Warner Protection Services, Cal State Fullerton, CB Commercial Property Management, Chrysler, City of Los Angeles, Columbia Health Network, Day Runner, Del Webb, Disney, Downey Savings, Fidelity National Title, First National Bank, Frontier Airline, General Mills, Globe Shoes, GSA, Indiana 1st Bank, Itochu International, Lawrence Berkeley Labs, Lexus, Lucent Technologies, Navigant International, Nightengale-Conant, Nokia, PacifiCare, PacifiCare Behavior Health, Parker Hannifin, Perkin-Elmer, Printronix, Prudential Insurance, Quantum ATL, Rain Bird, Scantron Corporation, Six Flaggs, Saint Mary's College, SBA, St. Luke Presbyterian Hospital, Swarthmore College, SuperShuttle, TCI, US West Communications, UCLA, UCI, Vans Shoes, VISA USA, Xerox plus an onslaught of initials of all the associations for which he's been a presenter. Associations like ABPA, AFSM, AHRMA, ARMA, BOMA, BRAMA, DMIA, MPI, NAED, NATSO, NBTA, NSRA, PIA, SAF, SITE, VSDA and WATSO.

Jeffrey earned his degree in 1979 from UC Irvine in psychology with a minor in biochemistry. His professional sales career began in 1980 as part of the exclusive Southern California Representative Firm for Apple Computer where he ended up being one of the top sales reps in the nation. Since then he's lead several companies to triple-digit growth as a senior executive and owned and sold his own international distribution company.

In 2001, he was awarded the Certified Speaking Professional (CSP) designation, the National Speakers Association. The CSP designation is the speaking industry's international measure of professional platform skill. Less than 7% of the 5,000 speakers who belong to the National Speakers Association and the International Federation for Professional Speakers hold this professional designation. It is earned by presenting at least 250 professional speaking engagements within a five year period, receiving excellent ratings from past clients on professional performance evaluations, continuing education in the professional speaking field, and subscribing to the Code of Professional Ethics of NSA and the IFPS.

Jeffrey Hansler is a member of the National Speakers Association, International Federation for Professional Speakers, National Speakers Association – Greater Los Angeles Chapter, and the American Society of Training and Development.

He has developed Directed Communication™, a sales communication process that follows the natural pattern of a conversation with a purpose. As a sales and negotiation expert, Jeffrey draws from two decades in communication to teach persuasive communication skills proven to break down barriers and build better relationships through the structure of language. His insights provide the critical link between hard closing and relationship selling.

He believes that if you "find your passions, you'll find success." He takes his passions and translates them into programs that encourage people to reach excellence. Clients describe his contributions as inspiring, humorous, memorable and above all, highly informative.

Jeffrey and his two sons make time for their passionate involvement in water polo, rugby, baseball, soccer, surfing, riding, and diving.

Call or email for more information on Jeffrey Hansler at

(714) 960-7461 • jhansler@oxfordco.com

http://www.oxfordco.com

Share It With Others
Quick Order Form

▣ **postal orders:**   Advantage Publishing Inc.,
9782 Hampton Ct, Fountain Valley, CA 92708

Please send more FREE information on:

❑ Speaking/Seminars ❑ Consulting ❑ Mailing Lists ❑ Reports

Name: _____

Delivery Address: _____

City: _____ State: _____ Zip: _____

Telephone: _____

email address: _____

Book Price: $20.00 single quantity

Shipping

U.S: $4.00 for first book and $2.00 for each additional copy.

International: $9.00 US for first book and $5.00 US for each additional

Payment: ❑ Cheque   ❑ Amex   ❑ Visa   ❑ MasterCard

Card number: _____

Name on card: _____Exp. date: _____

Telephone: _____

Address: _____

City: _____ State: _____ Zip: _____

Signature: _____

Orders with incomplete information will not be billed or shipped until completed. Allow 3-4
weeks for delivery.